BLOW HIGH, BLOW LOW
(From "CAROUSEL")

2nd TRUMPET

EDELWEISS
(From "THE SOUND OF MUSIC")

2nd TRUMPET

Lyrics by Oscar Hammerstein II
Music by Richard Rodgers

HONEY BUN
From ("South Pacific")

5

2nd TRUMPET

Lyrics by Oscar Hammerstein II
Music by Richard Rodgers

OH, WHAT A BEAUTIFUL MORNIN'
(From "OKLAHOMA!")

2nd TRUMPET

Lyrics by Oscar Hammerstein II
Music by Richard Rodgers

OKLAHOMA
(From "OKLAHOMA!")

2nd TRUMPET

Lyrics by Oscar Hammerstein II
Music by Richard Rodgers

YOU'LL NEVER WALK ALONE
(From "CAROUSEL")

2nd TRUMPET

Lyrics by Oscar Hammerstein II
Music by Richard Rodgers

*Legato phrasing throughout

ISBN-13: 978-1-4584-0161-8
Distributed By
HAL LEONARD
50488767
9 781458 401618

0 73999 88767 9

U.S. $9.99
HL50488767